COUNTING
CARDINALS

a memoir

TERRI SIGAFUS

Counting Cardinals
Published by Timber Wind Books
Copyright © 2016 Terri Sigafus
All rights reserved
ISBN 978-0-9779687-3-2
Library of Congress Control Number: 2015920680

No part of this publication may be reproduced, stored in or introduced into a retrieval system, or transmitted, in any form or by any means (electronic, mechanical, photocopying, recording, or otherwise), without the prior written permission of both the copyright owner and the above publisher of this book.

All scripture quotations are taken from the Holy Bible, *New International Version®, NIV®,* Copyright © 1973, 1978, 1984 by Biblica, Inc.™ Used by permission of Zondervan. All rights reserved worldwide.
Cover design by Nick Brimeyer

Printed in the U.S.A.

For additional information or to request an author visit, contact Timber Wind Books at www.countingcardinals.com.

For Kathy,
    for Susie,
        for Mom,
           for me …

Summer 2013

The Stillest of All Summers

It was the stillest of all summers.
Not a butterfly in sight.
The birds did not sing.
The maple tree in the front yard
stood tall
and sad
against the empty blue sky.
The summer Mom got sick.

The lilacs
I remembered from my youth,
once hearty,
vibrant,
looked pale,
frail ...
like Mom.

It was the summer of sadness—
      insufferable,
           inconsolable
                sadness.

It was the summer of laughter—
      joyful,
           triumphant
                laughter.

It was the summer that ended in silence—
    deafening,
        penetrating
            silence ...
as we laid Mom
to rest
in the shade of the oak tree,
in the quiet of the cemetery,
beside Grandma and Grandpa.
It was the stillest of all summers.

Bad News

It was a warm July afternoon,
the day I received the news.
"Mom has a brain tumor!"
my sister sobbed into the telephone.

No time to plan.
No time to think.
I threw some dirty clothes into a suitcase
and headed home
to Minneapolis,
after twenty-eight years of being away,
minus a handful of visits home on holidays.

My sister set out from Minneapolis.
Met us at the Missouri-Iowa border,
where my husband and I
said goodbye.
We traveled back to Minnesota,
Susie and I,
in awkward silence
at first.
Time does that.
Drives a wedge between people.
As we drove,
regret started gnawing,
like a dog on a fresh bone.

I began to ask myself *why*.
Why had I left home in the first place,
while my sisters stayed?

To start a new life.
To forget my old life.
To let bygones be bygones.
To marry Chad.
To be a mother.
To be a grandmother.

Suddenly the reasons seemed trite
as we traveled
in the dark of night,
through Iowa,
into Minnesota,
eating red licorice and jelly beans.

All the while
my insides screaming,
Please, God! Don't take our mother!
For Kathy,
    for Susie,
        for Mom,
           for me ...
for our peculiar little family.
Please, God!
Don't take our mother!

I Am Home

We pulled into Mom's driveway
just as darkness gave way to dawn,
first light casting its glow
on the corner
where I grew up.

The old neighborhood turned new.
Rows of tidy houses.
Two-car garages.
Neatly manicured lawns.
Sprinklers sprouting up
from the ground.
Everything altered
by the passing of time.

But not so much
that I could not picture
in my mind's eye
the little yellow house
that once
stood
on that corner.
Before the tornado
of 1984
blew it
away.

I could envision
the weeping willow
that overtook the front yard.
Feel its weedy branches
slide
between my fingers.

I see myself …
a little girl again,
      kneeling
            in the tall grass,
in a yellow cotton dress,
picking dandelions on Mother's Day.
A homemade card in my hand,
with a poem printed in purple crayon …
Mother my darling,
Mother my dear,
I love you,
I love you
Each day of the year.

Mom got teary
when I gave it to her.
She tucked it away,
in a shoebox under her bed.
I wasn't supposed to know it,
but I did.

I remembered the lilacs ...
    giggling,
        dancing,
            purple lilacs,
      fragrant,
hopeful.

The Lily of the Valley,
tiny,
delicate,
like lace,
growing along the shady side of the house.

Deep window wells
that smelled
of must,
with weeds climbing up and up,
and spiders lurking about.

Out back,
a run-down,
screened-in summer porch
that leaned against itself.
A fractured cement sidewalk
that wound its way
to the front door.

Inside were
small rooms,
linoleum floors,
a tattered armchair,
where Mom sat
in the wee hours of the morning,
drinking coffee
and writing numbers in a notebook.

Column after column,
page after page.
A mysterious mathematical complexity
she had been working on
for as long as I could remember.

I asked her once
about the numbers.
She just smiled
and kept writing.

Dad

When we were little,
Mom worked three jobs
to clothe and feed us.
Three little girls.
Three years apart.

Dad didn't help much.
He drifted in and out,
like a vagabond.
Couldn't hold down a decent job.
But he could sing.
Had a nice tenor voice.

Sometimes
late at night,
he would sneak
out the back door,
quiet as a mouse,
      hop the fence,
           take the car,
along with the grocery money from Mom's purse,
to go sing
in the nightclubs.

Mom would wake up
and find him gone.

Find the money gone ...
and cry.
I would sit beside her.
Hold her hand.
But I could not make it better.

The music bewitched him.
Ran feral through his veins ...
like a wild horse.
And it carried him
farther
  and farther
    and farther away,
      until he disappeared
        from sight.

Like Dad

After Dad left,
Mom carried on as best she could.
But wounded,
like a bird
with a broken wing.

After a while,
she got strong again,
and started taking night classes
to learn accounting.
Mom was clever with numbers.

I wanted to be like her.
But I had my father's forehead,
his restless spirit.
Mom loved me anyway.
Even when I reminded her of him.
How it must have hurt
to be reminded of him.

Lighthouse

Dark times settled in,
like the fogs of London.
But our little house glowed
from the inside out.
Like a lighthouse,
shooting beams of light,
razor sharp,
that cut through the murk
and the mist ...
through the shame
and disgrace
of fatherlessness.

Our little yellow house was my safe harbor.
And Mom was my lighthouse.

The Music

We had an old upright piano
in the living room.
It leaned
against a wall of knotty pine.
Had a rickety wooden bench
stowed beneath it,
stuffed full
of sheet music.

Mom could read the notes.
Turn them into music.
I wanted to learn.
She tried to teach me,
but I was too much like Dad.

The music ran wild through my head,
and out my fingers.
It would not be tamed.
So I pounded on the keys.

One day,
Mom bought me a child-size wooden guitar
with S&H Green Stamps.
I taught myself to play
and sing
Petula Clark songs.

And the music *became* me.
And I *became* the music.
I tamed the wild beast within.
Something Dad could never do.
For I was also
my mother's daughter.

Purple Crayon

Mom always laid our clothes out
for preschool the next day
at the Margaret Barry House,
where we took naps
on wobbly cots,
close to the floor,
in our underwear.

One winter morning,
Mom was upset.
Dad had lost another job.
Kathy left a purple crayon
in the pocket of her pants.

Mom ran it through the washing machine,
then the dryer,
with our white tee-shirts
and underpants.

The crayon melted.
Everything came out with purple stripes.

Mom cried.
I couldn't understand why.

Because purple was my favorite color,
and I didn't mind
taking naps
in purple-striped underwear.

Tornado

Mom was home alone
when it hit,
destroying everything in its path.
My sisters and I were away.
It was a wonder Mom wasn't killed.
God had other plans.

The insurance company paid
to build a new house
on the same corner,
with gold bricks,
a cement driveway,
fresh paint,
windows that opened and closed
and locked
from the inside.

As nice as it was,
it would never,
could never,
replace our little yellow safe haven.

Surprise!

Abruptly,
the memories scattered
as Susie pulled her SUV into
Mom's driveway.
In the time it took
to roll up the window,
open the car door,
and plant my feet firmly on the ground,
reality returned,
and I remembered
the reason I had come home
in the first place.

I yanked my suitcase from the back seat
and started up the walk.
The gentle glow from the lamp
beside Mom's chair
led the way.
She kept it lit
day and night.
A practice of living alone.

Mom had left the front door unlocked,
even though I had warned her
time and time again
not to do that.

I had phoned from a few blocks away
to announce my surprise visit.
Yet Mom was not surprised
that I had blown in,
like Mary Poppins
on the heels of the wind.

Something told me
she knew
I was coming.

Voices

Susie had wanted to keep it from her—
the results of the CT scan—
until it could be confirmed.
So I said nothing.
But I was never much good
at keeping secrets from Mom.

Mom and I talked
every day
on the telephone.
She had been complaining of dizzy spells.
I was a nurse.
"Nothing to worry about," I had said,
from seven hundred miles away.
I was wrong.

Mom did not stand to greet me.
Stayed seated instead.
In her armchair.
I wanted to hug her,
but our family didn't hug.
Never hugged.
But we loved.
Deeply loved.

I plopped down beside her.

I smiled.
She shrugged.
The way she did when she felt self-conscious.
From too many years of being judged
by voices
that whispered—
that made her feel small.
I used to hear them, too.
Sometimes,
I still do.

Hands

I reached over
and squeezed her hands.
Hands are like books.
They tell a lot about a person.
The lines and creases
unfold like a novel.

Mom's hands were happiest
when they were busy
crocheting
        mittens,
                hats,
                        scarves
for her children
and grandchildren.

Mom's hands had always been
thick and sturdy,
like man hands.
Good at fixing lawn mowers,
broken bicycle chains,
and electric sockets.

Other times
soft,
like silk,

when they played the piano,
brushed my tangled hair,
tied my shoelaces,
dried my tears.

No matter what,
Mom's hands
always took care of us.
Always.
We could count on Mom's hands
to pick us up
when we fell.

Now,
it frightened me
to see
those hands
lying restless
and uncertain
in her lap.

Nothing to Laugh About

When we were little,
we had a cat named Marshmallow.
He was big
and white.

One Christmas,
Mom knitted Marshmallow a red sweater.
It turned out too small.
When she put it on him,
he dropped to the floor
in a heap,
rolled onto his back,
and refused to get up.
Mom laughed.

Mom's laugh was soft,
like cotton balls.
And reserved,
so as not to call attention
to herself.

I would have given anything
to hear Mom laugh now.
But there was nothing funny
about brain cancer.

Trust in Jesus

I stowed my suitcase in the back bedroom.
Mom had turned it into an office.
I glanced around,
my eyes red,
gritty,
from lack of sleep.

On the desk,
beside the computer,
were photographs
in small mismatched frames,
of Kathy, Susie, and me.
Mom's little girls.

On the wall,
in a silver frame,
was a certificate
from the *Star Tribune* newspaper,
commemorating
thirty-five years of service.
A retirement gift from her co-workers.

I used to love to hear her tell the story
of when we had no money
to buy food
or clothes.

Mom had prayed the Rosary,
and the phone rang
with a job offer.
The *Star Tribune* needed a payroll clerk.
That's the first
I learned
about the power of prayer.

Mom worked hard
to climb
the ladder of success.
Went from payroll clerk
to Executive Director,
overcoming
paucity and shame.
And the whispering voices faded
into nothingness.
But they had left their mark behind …
like melting snow
on the tiny branch of a maple tree.
Bending it,
reshaping it,
but not breaking it.

On the office wall
adjacent to the certificate
was also a picture of Jesus Christ.
His robe glowing,

His face glowing
with
benevolence.

Trust in Jesus,
the inscription read …
but my heart
would not
be comforted.

I felt His eyes upon me
as I turned
and walked
away.

Church

When we were little,
we went to church every Sunday.
Wore doilies on our heads.
Sat in a pew near the back.
Dad on the end snoring.
My sisters and I giggling.
Mom in the middle nudging.

After Dad left,
we stopped going to church.
Because the voices
began to whisper.

Grandma still went
every day ...
to pray for us.
"God hears those good Catholic prayers,"
she always said.

When I got married,
I left the Catholic church.
Got re-baptized in a river.
When I came up,
the sun felt warm on my face,
and God's Spirit fluttered

inside me,
like a butterfly.

I felt clean
and new.
But Grandma disapproved
of my defection from the Catholics.

Mom didn't say much about it.
She just
      let me
           be me.

Kid Games

I returned to the family room
and sat down at the table.
It wasn't long before Mom
brought up
the dreaded subject of
the CT scan.

She asked me what I thought.
"Let's wait and see," I said.
Then turned my face away
before it could betray me.
Because I wanted so badly
to say
that everything would be
okay.
But I couldn't.

Instead,
I slipped off to the kitchen.
Made a pot of coffee.
I stood at the sink
gazing
out the window
at the neighboring back yards,
where the big empty field used to be—

remembering when we played
      baseball,
            kick the can,
                    red rover
with the neighborhood gang.
Back when kids could run wild
and not get kidnapped.

I used to love
to run
barefoot
through the tall grass.
Let the weeds tickle my elbows.
Watch the sun
inch its way across the endless blue sky.
No worries.
No cares.
Except to finish the ninth inning
before the sky turned orange
and Mom called us home for supper.
I'd toss the bat into the weeds
and race my sisters home
for spaghetti with meat sauce.

Why do people have to grow up?
Grow old?
And die?

Mom's Eyes

Once,
at the dinner table,
I dropped a pea into Susie's glass
and laughed out loud
when she spit milk
all over her plate.

Dad scolded me bad.
But Dad's scoldings didn't hurt.
Not like Mom's disapproving glance.

Mom could talk with her eyes.
They changed colors,
like a mood ring.

Most times,
they were soft and blue,
like the morning sky.
Other times,
hard and gray,
when a storm was stirring.

Susie and I shared a bedroom.
My side was always messy.
I couldn't see
over the piles of dirty clothes on the floor.

Mom would come in,
her eyes dark and rumbling,
like the billowing clouds
just before
a thunderstorm.

"Clean this room!" she would shout.
Then march off to cry somewhere
over something Dad had done.

I hated cleaning my room.
Grumbled
when she made me wash the dishes.
Stomped my feet
when she made me do laundry.
How I wish
now
that I hadn't.

A Visitor from Heaven

I stayed with Mom
while Susie ran errands for work.
That's what nurses do ...
stay with their patients.

Mom sat quietly in her chair,
staring
out the window.
I sat beside her.
I stared, too.

Before long,
a cardinal landed on the fence.
Mom turned to me,
her eyes soft, pastel blue ...
the color of the dishtowel
that hung
on the oven door.

She pointed to the little red bird.
"Cardinals are visitors from Heaven," she said.
"They come when we are sad or afraid."
"Who is it?" I whispered with childlike wonder.
"It's Grandma," Mom replied.

I was caught off guard.

I turned my head away,
determined not to cry.
But the tears fell anyway …
like soft summer rain,
down my cheeks,
down my neck.

The bird stayed
and sang
for the longest time,
before it flew away.

Big Sisters

Kathy came over that evening.
It was awkward
at first,
because
it had been so long.

When we were kids,
Kathy was wild and free,
like a mustang.
I was shy
as a rabbit.
I looked up to Kathy.
I wanted to be like her.

Kathy had her own room
and wouldn't let me in.
She and her friends smoked cigarettes
and listened
to Black Sabbath records.
But I didn't tell.

In ninth grade,
Kathy and her friends would trail me
down the third-floor hallway
of St. Anthony Village High,
chanting "*Va Gumba* …"

(I never knew what it meant.)
Then whack me with their hair brushes.
Still,
I didn't tell.

How is it that a big sister
can be
your archest enemy one minute,
and your hero
the next?

Because "blood is thicker than water,"
Mom used to say.
And the same blood flowed
through our veins.

My sisters and I
ate pizza
and drank wine.
And for the first time
since I'd arrived home,
I heard myself laugh.

When it came time for Kathy to leave,
I felt scared again—
like when I was little
and home alone.
Even though Susie had promised to stay.

That didn't count,
because
    Susie was
        littler than I.

Little Sisters

Some things never change …
like little sisters.

When Susie was young,
she had a face
round
as a berry
and peppered
with freckles.

She had a lisp.
Kathy and I used to tease her.
Mom got her speech therapy,
and the lisp went away.

Mom babied her anyway.
Made me play with her.
I would run
and hide,
but Susie always found me.

Kathy and I would trick her
into giving up her M&M's,
playing
"Which hand is it in?"

It seemed strange
to find
my little sister all grown up
into a successful professional,
with her world by the tail
and a confident smile.

Even so,
the scars of childhood remained.
They were etched into her soul,
like carvings on a stone,
yet hidden from plain view.
This I knew,
because
I had them, too.

Susie stayed that night,
and every night.
And during the day
when her work schedule would allow.
Even though she had a husband at home.
And we became companions.

I was grateful for this.
Because
I could not
have done it
without her.

One Day at a Time

Susie took the pull-out couch
in the living room.
It was bumpy ...
lumpy.
But we never told Mom that.
She was proud of her pull-out couch.

I took the recliner in the office,
and would lie
awake,
while the rest of the world slept,
watching
the street lights twinkle
through the blinds,
like little stars.

I would stare at Jesus on the wall,
and He stared back at me.
And I worried
about things to come.

Once,
just before I dozed off,
I heard God whisper to my heart,
"One day at a time, little lamb ...
one day at a time."

Hurt Feelings

Mom had a doctor's appointment
the following morning.
Susie and I scrambled for the shower
and the hair dryer,
like when we were teenagers.

Mom had been up since three o'clock,
sitting in her chair,
drinking coffee,
and writing numbers in her notebook.

She had dressed herself,
combed and curled her hair,
like nothing was wrong.

But on the way out the door to the car,
she nearly lost her balance.
I grabbed her arm.
She jerked it away,
scolding me with her eyes.
I stayed quiet
until she was safely buckled up
in the front seat.

Then I climbed into the back,
along with my hurt feelings.

We met Kathy
in the parking lot at the clinic.
Mom's regular doctor was away
on vacation.
How inconvenient.

The receptionist asked
to see Mom's insurance cards.
Mom fumbled clumsily with her wallet,
while the receptionist
drummed her fingers
impatiently
on the counter.

The four of us
were led
to a small examination room
to wait.
Finally—
a soft knock at the door.

The doctor
was a slight, middle-aged man
with poor posture
and a receding hairline.

He had a small voice
to match his stature.

I told him I was a nurse.
As if that mattered.
He acknowledged me with a nod,
but avoided my eyes.
Not a good sign.

He got right down to business.
"There are *two* large tumors in the brain," he said,
with such matter-of-factness,
as though reviewing plans for a room addition.
Pointing at the CT, he traced around them
with the tip of his pencil.

A jolt of adrenaline shot through me.
My heart began to pound
in my ears,
like kettle drums.
Tumors,
the size of walnuts,
were pressing
against Mom's cerebellum,
where balance was regulated.
It was a wonder Mom could walk at all.

I turned to view her reaction.
She was just gazing off,
like she was somewhere
far away.

Lake Johanna

When we were little,
Mom used to take us to Lake Johanna.
She'd load us up in the car
and we'd sputter off
down the road,
in our tired old jalopy,
leaving the unkempt lawn
to mow itself.
And we'd sing
to the radio,
KDWB,
and bounce
in the back seat
to the music,
all the way to the beach.

Then we'd pile out of the car,
and run,
     jump,
          play
in the soft, brown sand,
with plastic buckets and shovels,
while the waves washed up on the shore,
over our dirty feet.
Susie's chubby cheeks
spilled out

from the confines
of her yellow sunbonnet,
while Mom
reclined
in a rickety green lawn chair,
in her pale orange
one-piece bathing suit.

And we'd spend
all afternoon
building castles in the sand,
while Mom
gazed off ...

"I'm afraid there's nothing we can do,"
the doctor concluded.
My sisters and I exchanged worried glances.
And I was suddenly grateful
for the doctor's small voice,
for the simple reason
that Mom
had not heard him
over the sound of the waves
crashing against the shore
of Lake Johanna.

Nurses Don't Cry

My sisters walked Mom to the car
while I stayed behind
to ask the difficult questions.
Like, "How long?"
"Maybe four weeks," the doctor replied.
He suggested we call hospice.

He arranged for
a front-wheeled walker
with a seat
and a basket,
along with a referral
to the University of Minnesota Oncology Clinic
for palliative treatment,
to hopefully prevent seizures
as the cancer progressed.

As I gathered up Mom's sweater and purse,
I felt the doctor's hand touch my shoulder.
I looked up
into his pale green eyes.
"I'm sorry," he said.
But I turned my face away,
because nurses don't cry
in front of doctors.

House of Wong

Mom said she was hungry
for chow mein.
It was her favorite.

Kathy and I went for takeout.
Kathy broke down
behind the steering wheel of her car
in the parking lot
at the House of Wong.
It was hard
to see her that way,
because I had always seen her
as the stronger one.

I struggled
for something to say.
Mom's cardinal came to mind.
So I told her about it.
I thought it might help
if she knew
God had sent a cardinal
from Heaven.
"I don't believe in a God
who does such terrible things
to good people!" she sobbed.

I let it go,
let her cry,
and took my turn
being strong.

That night I prayed
for God
to send Kathy
a cardinal, too.

Amanda

A few days later,
hospice came.
I knew very little about hospice.
Only that they were the people you called
when all hope was gone.

They would bring
liquid morphine, Ativan, and Haldol.
And death always followed
in their footsteps.
I didn't want to,
but I let them in
anyway.

The nurse assigned to Mom's case was young.
In her mid-twenties,
with straight brown hair,
a slight smile,
and a small tattoo
on her right shoulder.
Her name was Amanda.

Mom hated strangers in her house.
I wasn't sure how this would go.
But Amanda made herself
at home.

She pulled up a chair and started talking
about her children,
     about her husband,
          about her dog,
in that order,
without any mention of
cancer
or dying.

Before I knew it,
she had wangled her way
into Mom's confidence,
and into mine.

With the touch of a hand
and a warm glow in her eyes,
she needed no words to say,
I'm here for you.
I'll be by your side
all through this journey.
And when it's over,
I'll still be here.

I walked Amanda to her car.
We stood in the driveway
for nearly an hour.
She listened
while I prattled on.

I was so relieved
to have someone to talk to,
someone who understood how I felt.
Because even though I was a nurse,
I was also a daughter.
And I was caught
somewhere in between.

Amanda smiled and nodded a lot,
and never once
looked
at her watch.

Before she left, she hugged me,
and I broke down
and sobbed into her tiny
tattooed shoulder.

Stranger Looking In

That weekend,
Kathy came
with her four girls.
Somehow,
they had grown up
when I wasn't looking.

They all sat
on the bedroom floor,
gathered around Mom,
going through boxes of old photographs,
our old report cards from elementary school,
and precious memorabilia
from days gone by.

Laughter filled the room
and spilled over into the hallway
where I stood,
braced against the door frame,
my arms folded
against my chest,
like a stranger looking in.

How could they laugh at a time like this?
Part of me longed
to laugh along with them,

but my heart
would not allow it.

No More Doctors

Monday came around,
and we set out
for
the University of Minnesota Oncology Clinic.
Maybe there was something *they* could do
to make things easier for Mom.

Susie's GPS malfunctioned.
We got lost.
Mom got nervous.
She hated being late.

When we finally arrived,
Mom started ramming around
with her rolling walker.
I could hardly keep up.
She pushed through the main entrance
into the crowded lobby,
like a fire engine into a busy intersection,
and collided
with a frail old man
who was also pushing
a rolling walker.

They locked wheels.
Around and around they went,

like ballroom dancers.
I struggled to separate them.
The old man laughed.
Mom laughed.
Even I laughed.

We hurried on
through the maze of tunnel-like hallways.
Left, right, left, right …
until we finally arrived at Radiation Oncology.

We were ushered down a long corridor,
to a small examination room
containing
one stainless steel exam table,
two metal chairs,
and a white ceramic sink.
The smell of antiseptic
lingered in the air,
like smoke
from burning leaves
on a Saturday afternoon
in October.

In teaching hospitals
doctors travel in flocks.
Like geese.
Only in white coats.

Before long,
the oncologist entered,
followed by four interns.
They squeezed into the small room
like college freshmen into a phone booth.
It was hard to breathe.

The doctor shook our hands.
"It's really quite remarkable
that your mother is doing so well,
under the circumstances ..."
She proceeded to inform me
that the most recent CT scan
revealed more than *twenty* brain tumors.
I needed time to process this.
But the doctor kept right on talking ...
"We'd like to map out her brain—
begin radiation right away,
before any seizure activity occurs ..."

A dreamlike silence ensued
as the oncologist stood waiting
for a reply.
All the while,
the interns were peeking out from behind her,
like little goslings from behind their mother.
Curious, no doubt,
as to how

Mom was still walking,
still talking,
with so many tumors
crowded inside her brain.

Mom turned to me,
her eyes a watered-down blue,
and I knew
she was tired.
"No more doctors," she said.
The nurse in me wondered,
Is this the right thing to do?
But Mom was firm.
"I just want to go home."

So we left the hospital,
having made a bad impression
because we would not do
what the doctor wanted.
And I worried
all the way home
that they might call Social Services on me.
Revoke my nursing license.
Even though I knew
that wasn't true.
Even if it had been,
I would not
have cared.

When It's Someone You Love

When someone you love
is diagnosed
with a terminal illness,
word travels
at the speed of light.

The well-wishers
pour out
of the woodwork,
with cards and flowers
and forced conversation,
driven by curiosity and fear,
because tragedy has struck so close to home.

The house gets loud and busy.
And the telephone rings off the hook.
And you eat pizza
until it's coming out of your ears.

Eventually,
the shock wears off.
The phone stops ringing.
And the well-wishers recede
into the woodwork.

And you're left with the day-to-day details

of caring for someone you love
who is sick
and dying.
The silence is deafening.

The earth continues to spin,
but your world
comes to a screeching halt.
Life rushes past you,
like a speeding car on the freeway.
You feel alone,
isolated,
frightened.

But you stay the course,
no matter how difficult the tasks at hand.
Because you love that someone.
And they're dying.
And they would do the same for you.

Some days you laugh.
Some days you cry.
Some days you're angry.
Some days you're scared.
You bounce so quickly
from one emotion to the next
that your head starts to spin
like a whirligig.

Sometimes,
you feel jealous,
because
the rest of the world has moved on ...
gone back to work,
out to lunch,
to dinner and a movie,
seemingly unaffected
by your tragedy.

And you begin to view death
as a mixed blessing,
because it brings
an end
to the pain and suffering ...

And then
you feel guilty,
and hate yourself
for having such thoughts.

So you stand strong,
even when you're not.
You learn to dodge and spar,
like a prize fighter.

Pick yourself up
when you get knocked down.

Climb back in the ring,
time after time.
Even though you're exhausted
and numb.
Even though
    you know
        you can't win this fight.

You do all this
because you love
that someone
so much,
that you can't imagine it
any
other
way.

Grandma's House

Each afternoon,
I would take a walk
to Grandma's house,
on Benjamin Street.

Grandma's house
was made of white stucco,
with tidy cement sidewalks
and a front door
made of dark, heavy wood,
with a window
for looking out.

As I passed by,
I was drawn in
by all that was familiar …
the crystal chandelier
that glistened
through the front window,
the geraniums and gladiolas
that bloomed in the front garden,
the branches of the birch tree
that rippled in the wind,
and waved to me,
like a childhood friend.

And every day,
I had to remind myself
that strangers
lived there now.

I would circle,
twice,
around the block.
Then cut through the alley
to get a better view
of the back yard,
where Grandpa used to sit
in his lawn chair
watering the grass,
and listening to the Twins
play baseball
on his transistor radio.

I did this every day,
because
there was
something about Grandma's house
that soothed my aching soul.

Soft as Red Velvet

When we were little girls,
Grandma took care of us.
When we were hungry,
she fed us.
When we were cold,
she warmed us.
When we were dirty,
she put us to soak
in her salmon-colored
ceramic bathtub.

On Easter Sundays,
I would help
shake out
the white lace tablecloth,
put fresh cut flowers in a vase
and colored eggs in a bowl.

Set the table
with delicate china plates,
and crystal glasses
that tinkled
when they bumped into each other.

Put matching silverware
all around,

from a wooden box
lined with soft, red velvet.

Grandpa would scramble eggs
and fry potatoes
in a cast iron skillet,
and sneak Buffy, their fat cocker spaniel,
little helpings
when Grandma wasn't looking.

Grandpa used to nudge me with his cane,
then look the other way,
pretending he hadn't.
Then chuckle softly to himself.
When Grandpa died,
Buffy died,
too.

Grandma could be awfully stern
at times.
But underneath her prickles,
she was as soft
as the red velvet
that lined her wooden silverware box.

Uncle Bobby

One day,
as I passed Grandma's house,
I heard a car horn honk.
I turned to find Uncle Bobby driving by.
"Want a ride?" he asked.
"No, thanks," I replied.
"I'd rather walk."

Uncle Bobby was Mom's older brother.
He lived nearby
and came to visit Mom every day.
Even before she got sick.

I would sit
and listen
to the two of them talk
about old times.
Mom this and Daddy that ...
They had the same color eyes.
Similar scars from past heartbreak,
having both survived bad marriages.
They were brother and sister,
but moreover,
they were good friends.

Uncle Bobby was quiet about Mom's illness.

He didn't ask many questions.
Which made me worry
that he might take it hard
when the time came.

And so we admitted Uncle Bobby
into our small circle of trust.
And he joined us on our journey
as we navigated
blindly
through the rugged terrain
of death
and dying.

Going Downhill

Deep into August,
Mom started going downhill.
At first she mixed up her words.
Then misplaced entire sentences.
Some days,
she said nothing
at all.

Other days,
she would fixate on things,
like buying a new washer and dryer.
Spend hours
poring over advertisements
in the newspaper,
asking me what I thought.

Mom started falling down—
in the bedroom,
in the hallway.
Got scraped and bruised.

Amanda told me
to stay close to her.
But the closer I stayed,
the madder Mom got.
She didn't like it

when I hovered.

Sometimes,
Mom would refuse to eat
and would sleep
the whole day away.
Then be up all night,
writing numbers in her notebook.

I didn't want her to be alone,
so I fought to stay awake.
All the while
I couldn't help but notice
that her columns
were leaning.

The Rosary

During the day,
I kept the TV tuned to the Catholic station,
so Mom could watch and listen
to Sister Angelica
and the nuns
recite the Rosary.

At night,
I kept the radio beside her bed
on the Catholic programs,
so she could listen to Mass.

Mom had a string
of powder-blue rosary beads
on a silver chain.
She kept them under her pillow,
or in the pocket of her pajamas.

Sometimes,
she would reach into her pocket
and touch them,
but not take them out.
Until she went to bed.
Mom was private
about her prayers.

In the morning,
when I made her bed,
I would find her rosary beads
tangled
in the sheets,
and would slip them
back into her pocket,
without her knowing it.

I often wondered
what she and God
talked about.

The Healing Sacrament

Susie had arranged
for the priest to come
and give Mom the Last Rites.
But they don't call it that anymore.
Instead,
they call it
the Healing Sacrament.

Father Brian knocked at the door
on a Wednesday afternoon.
I guessed him to be
in his early thirties—
tall and thin,
with dark curly hair
and a winsome smile.
A pleasant and gregarious fellow.
A new breed of priest.
Not like I remembered.

Susie and I met him at the door
and quickly pulled him into the living room
to brief him privately on Mom's condition.
We told him not to expect much,
because she was very sick.

The next thing I knew,
Mom entered the room
pushing her rolling walker,
her eyes a vibrant blue,
her cheeks red
as rosy posies.

Father Brian surely thought
Susie and I
were alarmists.

The priest settled into a chair
across from Mom
and listened intently
as she confessed
to having missed many Masses.
But, she assured him,
she still gave money to the church,
and to St. Jude's Hospital, too.

Father Brian suggested we move on
to the Healing Sacrament.
I held my breath as Mom lowered herself
to her knees.
"Let us pray," said Father.

But the proceedings came to a screeching halt
when Mom blurted out,

"My daughter isn't a Catholic anymore!"
All eyes fell upon me.
"But Mom, I'm still a Christian!" I protested
in my own defense.
"I think she can still pray with us," Father Brian said,
tossing me a sideways smile.

So Mom received the sacrament,
and literally glowed
for the next week.
It was all she talked about,
until the tumors
gobbled up
the memory.

Deferred

As September grew nearer,
Mom drifted farther away.
She sat
quietly
in her chair,
writing numbers in her notebook.
Except they didn't look
much like numbers
anymore.
Just scribbles on the page.

She fell a few more times.
Got scraped and bruised.
But never cried.
Except for once,
when she tried to curl her own hair
and burnt her forehead
on the curling iron.

I stuck close to Mom,
even though
it made her angry.

Sometimes,
she would get so furious
that she would throw

knitting needles,
forks,
and calculators at me.
I got really good
at dodging flying objects.

Amanda blamed Mom's anger
on the brain tumors.
But I blamed myself
for everything.

When things got out of hand,
I would call Kathy,
because
she always knew
what to do.
All it took sometimes
was a different face
to calm Mom down.

It got to the point where
Kathy was coming every evening.
We would sit,
Kathy, Susie, and I,
in the family room
and talk,
while Mom just listened.

One evening,
Mom got a big burst of energy
and started saying
the same word
over and over.
The word was *deferred*.
And she would laugh out loud,
like she had just told the most hilarious joke,
which made us laugh, too—
so hard
that we nearly rolled on the floor.
Mom had the most contagious laugh.

My Songs

When Mom couldn't walk anymore,
I sat her on the seat of her rolling walker
and pushed her
from the bedroom
to the family room,
and back again.

We did this
over
and over ...
sometimes, all day long.
It made us both feel
like we were accomplishing something.

When Mom got too weak to stand,
I used a gait belt to transfer her.
One day,
while moving her from the bed to the chair,
we went down—
both of us.
And landed on the floor
in a heap.

I thought about running
to a neighbor for help,
but I didn't want to leave her alone.

Somehow,
I managed to get her
back into bed.

I could tell by her eyes
she was scared.
So I sang her a song.
She closed her eyes
and smiled.

I used to think
Mom didn't like my songs.
I was wrong.

The End Begins

The next night,
I dragged the recliner
from the office
into Mom's bedroom,
to be close to her as she slept.

I woke up
to find her thrashing around in bed,
crying out, "Mom! Mom!"
Like she was looking for Grandma.

I called hospice
and was instructed to give her
morphine and Ativan every four hours.
I was afraid I would accidently kill her.
But I did it anyway.

Amanda came the following morning
to check on us.
Mom was up in her chair,
giggling like a drunk sailor
from the drugs.

Amanda suggested calling for a nurse's aide
to give Mom a bath.
I declined.

Mom was too modest for that.
"I'll do it," I said.

After Amanda left,
I wheeled Mom into the bathroom,
sat her on the edge of the tub,
and turned on the water.
She ordered me *OUT!*

I slipped around the corner
and watched
through the crack in the door
as Mom pulled off her pajama top
and dipped it in the bath water.
Then wrung it out
like a wet towel.
All the while,
humming
cheerfully.
I couldn't help but smile.

I Love You

A few days later,
Mom got restless and agitated again.
She wouldn't eat
or drink.

I called Amanda.
She instructed me to increase the frequency
of the drugs,
to keep Mom calm and comfortable.
I reluctantly agreed.

Later, while Mom slept,
my sisters and I sat in the family room
and talked things over.
We did lots of crying,
lots of laughing,
ate lots of pizza,
and drank lots of wine.
And I realized
how much I missed my sisters
and my old home.

Yet I was homesick
for my husband
and my family
at the same time.

Nearly five weeks had passed
since I'd seen them.
I thought I was ready for this journey to end.
But I wasn't really.

Mom got more agitated with each passing day.
Amanda told me to give her the drugs
even more frequently.
They knocked Mom out,
just like I worried they would.

I got scared again
that I would kill her,
so I sat
at the foot of her bed
and watched her sleep.

Before long,
she opened her eyes
and said,
"You've always been my worrier …"
Then she drifted off again.
I thought she was gone,
until I saw the steady rise and fall
of her chest.
I was relieved.

I crawled into bed beside her,

took a deep breath.
I breathed in the smell of her hair ...
of her skin,
so I would never forget what she smelled like.

I studied Mom's face ...
every line,
every wrinkle,
and marveled
at how beautiful
my mother was.

"I love you, Mom," I whispered.
"I'm sorry that I left.
I'm sorry that you're sick ...
I'm sorry that you're dying ...
I'm sorry for everything
I ever did,
or said,
to hurt you ..."
And I sobbed into her neck,
into her hair,
and prayed
that God would give me a sign
that Mom had heard me.

Within the hour,
my prayer was answered.

Mom opened her eyes
and said,
"I love you, too."

The Last Time

The next day,
Uncle Bobby stopped by.
Mom opened her eyes
just long enough to say a few words
in private.
Uncle Bobby left with tears in his eyes.

Then Mom asked to be alone.
She wanted to sit up in her recliner.
I positioned her head
on a small pillow,
and pulled her cranberry afghan
up
over her legs.

She looked up at me,
a faint smile on her lips.
That was the last time
I looked
into my mother's eyes.

I held her hand in mine
and studied it.
Her once nimble fingers
were now riddled with purple veins
that looked like they would pop through her skin.

Her mother's ring
hung loose,
and spun
on her finger,
like a horseshoe around a metal stake.

She had grown old
while I was looking away.
And there was no
turning back
the hands of time.

I must have told her
a thousand more times
that I loved her,
hoping she would open her eyes
just once more …
but she didn't.

Cheers

My sisters and I
dragged kitchen chairs
into Mom's bedroom,
along with a bottle of wine.

We gathered around her.
We laughed.
We cried.
We toasted her life.
We talked about Heaven,
about God,
and read the Bible together.

Kathy asked me how long it would be.
I said I didn't know.
I said maybe there was a traffic jam up there,
and Mom was circling …
and we laughed
hysterically.

Fly Away

I read somewhere
that when a person's body is broken
beyond repair,
the spirit leaves
and hovers over the room,
watching
and waiting,
to be sure
their loved ones are okay …
before they fly away.

Mom flew to Heaven at 9:02 that evening,
while we were sharing stories,
laughing,
and drinking wine.

Guido and Knuckles

When the undertakers arrived
in their black suits,
with their hair all slicked down,
they looked like
hoodlums
from the Italian Mafia.
Kathy nicknamed them
Guido and Knuckles.

They were carrying a
      large
            black
body bag.
I led them down the hall to Mom's room
and left them to their task.

I was okay
until they nearly dropped her
on their way out.
Then I fell to pieces.
Because it suddenly hit me
that Mom
was never coming back.

I wailed violently.
I wanted to run after them.

Make them give her back.

I would have gladly
gone through it all
again,
and again,
if only
they would give her back.

Kathy and Susie tried to console me,
but I was inconsolable.
Kathy led me to the pull-out couch,
ordering me to lie down.
Then she crawled in
beside me
and put her arms around me.
Susie crawled in
beside Kathy,
and we all three lay there
together,
on Mom's pull-out couch ...
Mom's lumpy,
bumpy,
pull-out couch.
Like frightened little girls
waiting for Mom to come home.

She's Everywhere

It took two days for my family to arrive
from Missouri.
I rushed out to the curb
to greet them.
Chad put his arms around me.
For the first time in five weeks,
I felt safe.

Mom's house
grew loud and lively again
with preparations for her funeral.
But as evening fell,
the house grew eerily quiet.

I found my daughter
Addie
sitting alone on the couch,
her eyes moist and red.
I sat down beside her.
"I can feel Grandma everywhere in this house,"
she said,
her lips trembling.
I wrapped my arms around her,
and we both
broke down
and cried.

Streamers and Egg Noodles

The funeral home called,
requesting that we come
to view Mom's body.
To make sure everything was okay.

When we arrived,
we found Mom
in a back room,
surrounded
by colorful streamers hanging
from the rafters,
and plates of leftover egg noodles.

Naturally,
we inquired as to why.
The funeral director explained
that they had run out of rooms
and had no other place
to put her.
But, he assured us,
Mom had not been present
for the Vietnamese funeral
that had taken place
earlier that day.

I think Mom would have found
the whole thing
amusing.

I could almost
hear her laugh.

Laying Mom to Rest

I sat
in the third pew at the church,
in the seat nearest to the aisle.
Close enough to reach out
and touch
Mom's casket.
But I didn't.

She would have been proud,
because everyone came.
People she knew from work,
friends from the village,
close and distant relatives …
all because
they loved her.

Except for Dad,
who had called two days earlier,
asking if he could sing
at the funeral.

I didn't think
Mom would approve.
I said no.
Kathy and Susie said no,
too.

I guess we offended him,
because he never did
show
up.

After the Mass,
the funeral director
removed Mom's ring
and handed it to me,
and gave Mom's rosary beads
to Susie.

We joined in the long procession of cars
en route
to the cemetery.

It was a still summer day
when we laid
Mom
to rest
in the shade
of the oak tree,
beside Grandma and Grandpa.

I hated putting her in the
hard,
dark
ground.

But the Bible says
to be absent from the body
is to be present with the Lord.
And I knew she wasn't
here
anymore.

We left the cemetery,
and returned to the church
for
turkey sandwiches
and tortellini salad.

Guido and Knuckles were there
wearing dark sunglasses,
and spooning large portions of food
from the buffet table
into takeout containers.

Kathy later told me
she had spied
a black eye
behind Guido's Foster Grants.

Mowing by Moonlight

The drive home to Missouri was a blur.
Except for when we pulled
into our driveway,
and I jumped out of the car
and ran for the lawn mower.
I mowed the lawn by moonlight.
I'm not really sure
why.

Waiting for a Cardinal

I returned to my job at the nursing home
a few days later.
Looking back,
it was probably too soon.

I received
a letter from Amanda,
asking how I was doing.
I never answered.

I caught myself
staring out the window a lot,
looking
for a cardinal.
But no cardinal came.

My husband hung a bird feeder
out back,
hoping to attract the hearty red songbird.
Still no cardinal came.

Each night,
I prayed for a cardinal
to show me that Mom was okay,
that she had made it to Heaven.
But my prayers went unanswered.

Until one afternoon,
when I passed the room of an elderly woman,
who was dying
alone.

I entered her room
and sat down beside her.
As I gently stroked her hand,
I leaned over and whispered softly,
"Soon, you'll be going to Heaven.
My mom lives there.
She's tall with soft blue eyes.
Please ask her to send me a cardinal."

The woman did not respond.
But I stayed at her bedside anyway,
for as long as I could.
Because nobody
should have to die
alone.

Inundated

The following day was Saturday.
I had been up about an hour
when my husband called me to the front porch.
I could not believe my eyes.
There in the tree
was a cardinal.
A big, red cardinal!

Chad ran for his camera.
The bird stayed
and let him take lots of pictures.
For the first time
since returning home,
I heard myself laugh.

Later that morning,
I phoned the nursing home
to check on the elderly patient.
The charge nurse informed me
that she had passed away.

Over the next few weeks,
I was inundated with cardinals.
I counted more than twenty
in our back yard at one time.

I texted photographs
of the cardinal sightings
to my sisters in Minnesota.
They messaged back,
saying
they were happy for me,
but regrettably
had not yet
seen any cardinals
there.

A Call from Heaven

A few weeks later,
the cardinals stopped coming.
I was disappointed.
I moped around
like a spoiled child.

I slowly backslid
into depression,
started crying myself to sleep,
disengaged from family members
and friends,
grew distant from co-workers.
I refused to go places
or see people.
I was caught in a tailspin
and could not pull out of it.

Christmas was quickly approaching.
But I was in no mood for folly.
I was simply existing ...
drifting
from one day to the next,
wishing
I could talk to Mom
just one more time.

One night,
I dreamed I heard the phone ring.
I picked it up.
Mom was on the other end.
She said,
"Hi, Hon. I'm fine. It's beautiful here.
You'll be okay. Just stay
on sixty-one …"

I begged her not to hang up.
But she said she had to go,
and ended
the call.

I shot up in bed,
wondering if it was real
or a dream …
because it felt too real
to be a dream.

I called my sisters the next day
and told them about the call from Heaven.
They were as puzzled as I was.
None of us had any idea
what sixty-one meant.

From the Ends of the Earth

Shortly after Christmas,
I received a visitor in my office.
The sister of a patient
had come
to say
that God woke her up
in the middle of the night
with a message for me.
She had written it down
and brought it straight over.

I unfolded the note
and could not believe my eyes.
It read *Psalm 61:2.*

I caught up with the woman in the hallway.
"How did you know about Mom ...
about sixty-one?" I insisted.

The woman said
she had no idea
that my mother had passed away,
and knew nothing of sixty-one.

Before we parted,
she looked into my eyes and said,
"Don't be sad.
Your mother has run the race
and is now at peace."

She spoke with such authority
that I could not help
but feel
she was speaking for God.

I went
in search of a Bible,
and found one
in the first room I came to.
It was lying open …
to Psalm 61.

I read verse 2.
"From the ends of the earth I call to you,
I call as my heart grows faint;
lead me to the rock that is higher than I."

Counting Cardinals

From that day forward,
I began to heal.
The tears still found me,
but not everywhere.

Some days,
I miss Mom
so much
that I can't breathe.

Some days,
I wonder who I am
without her.

Then I look in the mirror
and see
her looking back at me …
reminding me
that I am
my mother's daughter.

I see her smile,
hear her laugh,
in my sister
Kathy.

I see her courage,
her determination
in my sister
Susie.

Since Mom left,
I've counted hundreds
of cardinals.
Even now, as I pen these words,
a cardinal sits in a nearby tree,
watching me …
      reminding me
that Mom has merely gone before me—
that we will see each other again,
and sit side by side
counting cardinals
forever.

The End

Counting Cardinals is also available in a children's version, written by Terri Sigafus and illustrated by Rebekah Sigafus. For additional information, contact Timber Wind Books at www.countingcardinals.com.

The Smith Family

Mom

Kathy

me

Susie

CPSIA information can be obtained
at www.ICGtesting.com
Printed in the USA
FFOW02n0711030817
38247FF